# CRESCENT HOME WORKSHOP

# PICTURE FRAMING

## SONIA AARONS

# ❧ CRESCENT HOME WORKSHOP ❧
# PICTURE FRAMING
## SONIA AARONS

CRESCENT BOOKS

NEW YORK • AVENEL, NEW JERSEY

# *Home Workshop*
# PICTURE FRAMING

**4**

Page 2: A grouped assortment of the framer's art.

This 1994 edition published by Crescent Books,
distributed by Outlet Book Company, Inc.,
a Random House Company,
40 Engelhard Avenue, Avenel, New Jersey 07001

RANDOM HOUSE New York • Toronto • London • Sydney • Auckland

Copyright © 1994 Harlaxton Publishing Limited
Copyright Design © 1994 Harlaxton Publishing Limited
2 Avenue Road, Grantham, Lincolnshire, NG31 6TA, United Kingdom.
A member of the Weldon International Group of Companies.

Publisher: Robin Burgess
Design and Coordination: Rachel Rush
Editing: Martyn Hocking
UPS Translations UK
Illustrator: Jane Pickering
Photography: Chris Allen, Forum Advertising Limited
Typesetting: Seller's, Grantham
Color Reproduction: GA Graphics, Stamford
Printing: Imago, Singapore

Title: Crescent Home Workshop - PICTURE FRAMING
ISBN: 0-517-08778-2

*Home Workshop*

# CONTENTS

Everyone has a favorite picture they have been meaning to frame. It could be a family photograph, a needlepoint completed after many hours of work, a sketch of your own, a watercolor picked up at a local swap meet or art exhibition, a poster given for Christmas, or simply a picture cut from a magazine that has caught your eye. Put a frame around it and it is transformed and becomes a focal point.

A framed picture can find a home in any room of the house, even the bathroom or kitchen. Some of the most interesting anecdotes and events from people's lives are recorded on the walls of the downstairs restroom! A framed print of your favorite cartoon will cheer you every time you see it; a collection of humorous items grouped together is even better and makes good alternative reading! Rather than pin your children's paintings on the kitchen cabinets, why not frame them for their bedrooms?

*Picture Framing Home Workshop* shows you step-by-step how to make the best of your pictures. From choosing the right style of frame and color matt (the cardboard border), through to cutting the molding, matt, and glass. For the more ambitious, *Picture Framing Home Workshop* shows how to create eye-catching, decorative effects with painted frames and matts with attractive borders.

Using the right equipment correctly is important if you are to achieve a satisfactory end result. A badly-made frame and poorly-cut matt will immediately detract from the picture, reducing its impact.

*Picture Framing Home Workshop* describes everything you will need to do-it-yourself; types of molding, glass, matt boards, hanging accessories, and how to use the specialized tools like a matt-cutter and miter box or saw.

Once you have achieved a simple picture frame and matt you may like to extend your creative talents to specially-finished frames, decorated with unusual effects such as tortoise shelling and marbling. The matts, too, can be decorated quite easily and *Picture Framing Home Workshop* shows you the various ways this can be done.

Never think your picture is not worth framing, but remember it will benefit from being carefully hung. A single small picture hung too high on a large wall will look lost while, oddly enough, a large picture on a relatively small wall can look stunning. *Picture Framing Home Workshop* will help you make the most of your pictures once they are framed, with ideas for hanging arrangements. So, where did you put that nice print that a favorite aunt gave you for Christmas?

OPPOSITE: Framed pictures can add style and a finishing touch to any room in the home.

# *Home Workshop*
# GETTING STARTED

Framing does not need a special workroom, just
a good-size work surface and room to move
lengths of molding and sheets of glass safely.

## MAKING ROOM

It may appear the most convenient place, but really the dining-room table is not always
the best for framing, particularly if it is a small room. Lengths of molding can be supplied
up to 10ft long and if you have to cut this length or even half that, maneuvering can be
tricky ... and possibly fatal for anything delicate on the shelf behind you!

You will need to clamp the miter box or saw to the surface you are using – a well-
polished table would not appreciate it. A kitchen table would be a better choice and you
could cover the surface with a piece of chipboard ensuring first that the table is protected by
a cloth or an old sheet. Make sure the board is secure and overlaps the table beneath.

Ideally, choose a room where if need be the molding can pass through a window or a
door; alternatively you could cut the frame roughly to size in a garage or outdoors. You will
also need space to safely handle a large sheet of glass if you are not having it cut to size, as
well as room to put all the materials you need conveniently to hand. A shelf or cart placed
close by to hold the equipment you are going to be using is always helpful.

Make sure that you will have room to lay a frame down on the table without it hitting the
wall and that the floor can be swept easily (ideally it should be covered with tiles or vinyl).
Sawdust, glue, and paint stains are the main hazards.

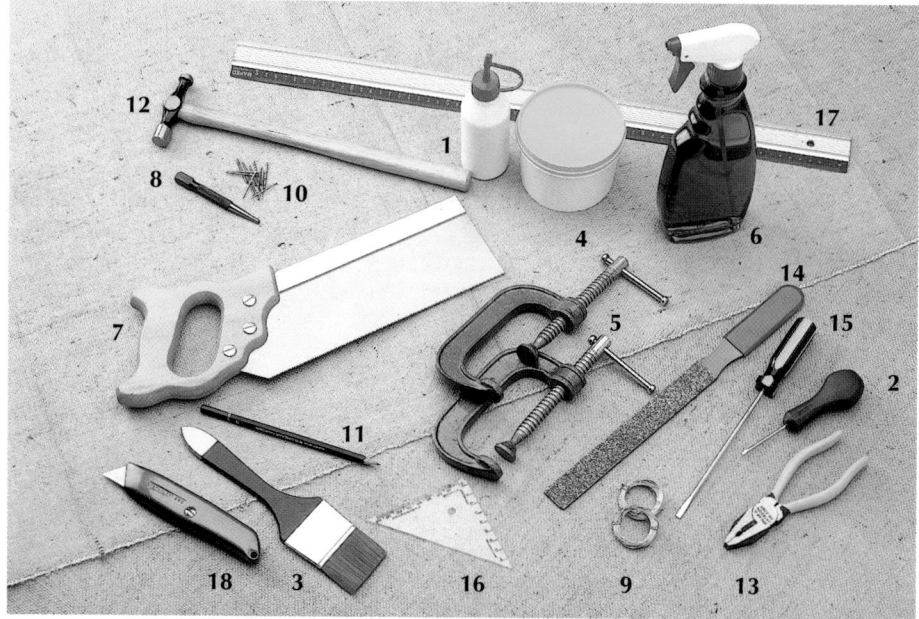

## EVERYDAY TOOLS

Y ou will need to gather some basic tools to start with:

1: ADHESIVE – strong and quick drying wood glue, for joining corners.

2: AWL – for drilling pilot holes for picture hanging fittings.

3: BRUSH – to keep dust away from the picture and glass.

4: FILLER – for minor repairs.

5: G-CLAMPS – for holding molding and miter-box, if used, in place.

6: GLASS-CLEANER – to remove stains and fingerprints from the glass surface.

7: MITER-SAW OR TENON-SAW – which does not whip around as much as a handsaw.

8: NAIL PUNCH/SET – for driving in panel pins.

9: NYLON CORD OR PICTURE WIRE – for hanging the frame.

10: PANEL PINS – for pin fastening and joining.

11: PENCIL – a soft pencil for marking.

12: PIN HAMMER – with a suitable size and type of head.

13: PLIERS – for cutting picture framing wire and to remove pins if necessary.

14: RASP – for chamfering rough edges of backboard.

15: SCREWDRIVER – for attaching fittings.

16: SET SQUARE – for checking that joints are square.

17: STRAIGHT EDGE – a steel ruler.

18: TRIMMING KNIFE – with replacement or snap-off blades is best.

### SPECIAL TOOLS

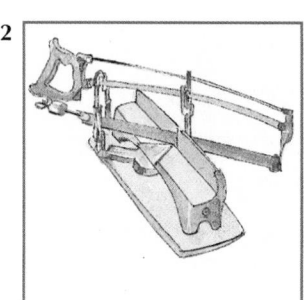

You will also need some items you are unlikely to find in the toolbox. Many of the tools for picture framing are simple, inexpensive, and easily available.

Some can only be found in art or framer's stores and, depending on whether you are likely to frame just one picture or a number over a period of time, you will need to decide how much you are prepared to spend.

### Mitering Equipment

In particular, there is a choice in mitering equipment. You will need a miter of some type to cut accurate corners for your frames.

Nothing ruins the look of a frame more than poorly-cut corners which do not meet and sad to say, even some professional framers are at fault here, simply because they use blunt equipment.

1 The simplest is a miter-box used with a miter-saw or tenon-saw. This has two angled cuts into which you place the saw and you can achieve reasonable results as long as the box is held firmly clamped to the workbench and the molding is also held in place.

2 A larger investment, but well worth it if you are proposing to make several frames, is a miter-saw. These are marked with constant cutting angles, normally of 45° as well as others suitable for making many-sided frames, even hexagons if you get really ambitious!

Miter-saws will also adapt to the depth of the molding (some will cut wood up to six inches deep) and have built-in clamps to ensure the molding is held firmly in place. The saw itself has a clamp to secure it to the working surface.

## Glass Cutters

A good glass cutter is essential if you are to attempt cutting your own glass to size. Alternatively, you can ask your dealer to cut the glass once you have the frame and matt ready. The best type of glass cutter, used by professional framers, has a handle which contains oil. This constantly lubricates the blade and prevents it from heating up and becoming blunt, also helping it run more smoothly.

**Most hardware stores sell a simple glass-cutter, which should be lubricated with cutting oil or white spirit. With practice (this is an acquired talent), you can achieve good results with these.**

## Clamps

To make up the frame, you will need a means of holding the four sides together. To do this, you could use four corner-clamps or a specially-made set of clamps linked by a tape. One corner includes a winding mechanism which allows you to adjust the tape linking all four corners. This means you can clamp all the corners together at once and tighten or loosen the tape according to the size of the frame and the pressure needed.

## Staple Guns

Professional framers favor an alternative to hammering in panel or veneer pins to hold the hardboard backing in the frame. They use a gun which shoots diamond or arrow-shaped, flat metal tabs into the inside edge of the frame rabbet so that it traps the glass, cut matt, original picture, and hardboard backing in a "sandwich".

# *Home Workshop*
# CHOOSING
# A MOLDING

Y ou will probably be able to buy your
molding from an art store or professional
framer's, although some wholesale suppliers
may be prepared to sell you the odd length.

W hile there are thousands of wooden moldings to choose from, metal frames can be
supplied cut to size. Metal frames, which can look great around modern posters, are
now available in a wide variety of colors and finishes, although they tend to be limited in
design. They are put together with special screw-fittings so they are simpler to assemble.

However, there is a far greater variety of wooden frames to suit all types of pictures and
you will have a good deal of fun making up your mind. Be prepared to spend some time
doing this! Bear in mind that you will need to choose the color of the matt cardboard at the
same time, so take your picture with you.

## CHECKING THE DEPTH

M oldings vary in depth, so you will need to make sure when you choose the frame that the rabbet is able to accommodate your picture, matt, plus the hardboard, plus the glass (if any).

Needlepoint and oil paintings can cause particular difficulties if the molding is not deep enough and you may need to increase the depth of the rabbet of the frame with additional wood. It is not necessary to use glass with oil paintings nor with some kinds of needlepoint.

There are many attractive frames to choose from. Pastel colors and light, plain woods are very popular and in keeping with today's lighter decor. Bold primary colors as well as black, silver, traditional gold, and darker plain wood are also available; increasingly chosen for their simplicity are natural wood moldings including pine, hickory, and redwood along with plain woods suitable for decoration, which will be discussed later. These can also look stunning if simply limed and polished.

BELOW: A selection of attractive wood and metal moldings.

## COMPLEMENTING THE PICTURE

Embossed designs, both plain wood and gilded, are ideal for complementing traditional landscapes, but try not to combine too elaborate a frame with a fussy or busy picture.

Where possible, choose a shade from the picture which can be highlighted by the frame. What is known as a gold slip may be of use to lighten a darker wooden frame. A thin strip of wood, usually in gold but available in other shades too, called a slip, sits inside the main frame. Slip is sold in lengths which can be mitered just like normal molding.

On occasion you may find it useful to buy a ready-made "swept" frame. These are the traditional-style prefabricated gilt frames (also available in plain or stained wood, oak, mahogany, and so on) which are made to standard sizes and often suit oil paintings and mirrors. They are available in both rectangular and oval shapes.

## BUYING MOLDING

You should make allowances, when buying molding, for the amount you will lose when cutting a miter and for making a test cut or two; as mentioned earlier, the ends of the molding may have to be trimmed back before you can use it. Ideally, buy it to the nearest foot, or add a foot or so to the final figure.

To work out the final length needed, first measure the length and width of the artwork or the outside of the matt, if you are using one. Add $1/8$in to each measurement just to ensure the artwork and matt will not be too tight in the frame. Then add the length of each piece, including the allowance, which will give you the measurement of the frame. Then find the width of the molding, multiply it by eight (for eight miters) and add this figure to the figure for the perimeter of the framed item. Then add on the cutting allowance.

When you choose the molding, ensure the lengths you buy match as closely as possible; colors can vary, as can the width. Also check that the molding is not bent, damaged, or warped in any way.

ABOVE: Examples of "swept" frames.

## HOW TO CUT MOLDINGS

W hen faced with a 10ft length of molding (although smaller lengths are available) it is tempting to ask your supplier to cut it up. If possible, avoid doing this; you will inevitably end up with pieces of molding you cannot use or which are not quite long enough for what you want.

1 If you are using a miter-box, hold the wood firmly (it may be helpful to wedge a bit of cardboard under the rabbet to make it firm).

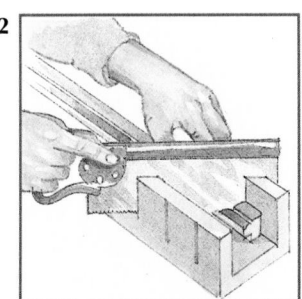

2 With the rabbet against the far inside of the miter box and with the face of the frame upward, cut the first miter. You should cut about 3/8in from the end of the molding to make sure you cut the complete angle and to avoid the rough ends of the molding.

3 Mark each length on the back in pencil as you cut it, 1 and 2 (the long sides), then 3 and 4 (the short sides). Do not try and mark it all at once – work on each length one at a time.

Some woods are softer than others so make sure you saw firmly but without forcing, which may crush the wood. Measure the length of the first leg (cut the long sides first – you can always cut them down if you make a mistake).

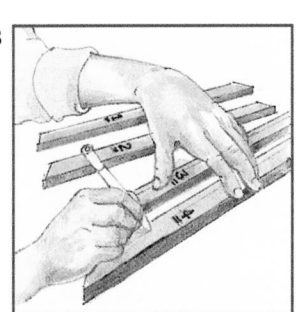

4 Mark the length in pencil on the molding, measuring along the outside edge, and cut to the pencil line, using the appropriate angle and ensuring the back of the molding is at the far edge of the miter-box.

5 Once you have cut length 1, you can use this to show exactly where the second miter should end on length 2. Put the two lengths together so they make a shape like the bow of a ship and mark the miter on 2. Cut it in just the same way as the first.

6 Repeat the process for 3 and 4 – the two short sides.

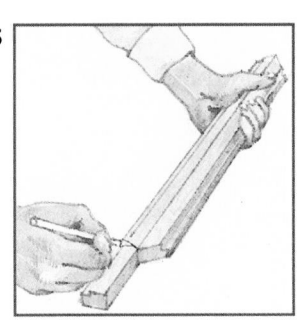

OPPOSITE: Samples of mitered moldings.

Do not sand the rough ends of the miters. If you do this, they may not fit together correctly. The edges can be smoothed very gently with fine glass-paper wrapped around a sanding block, or remove the rough bits with a craft- or trimming-knife. Keep checking that you are not altering the shape, by putting the two ends together and ensuring they make a neat, clean line – you should hardly see the join (hopefully!) when the frame is finished.

The extensive range of matts (also known as mounts) will enable you to select a color, the core (revealed when the bevel is cut) and even the texture of board to suit your picture.

**B**oards with a black or colored core instead of the normal white/cream core, can provide a readymade border when the bevel is cut – often very effective with black-and-white photographs.

You may also wish to decorate the matt, in which case you will need to think about the color coordination of any rules or borders you wish to add.

You can achieve a similar effect by cutting a double matt, using two boards in complementary colors, one cut to give a narrow border inside the other.

Some boards reflect the stippled effects often used as paint techniques, while others have a textured finish rather than being smooth.

If you are framing a valuable picture, a watercolor, or sketch, it is advisable to choose a conservation or acid-free type of board to prevent any discoloration of the picture as the board ages.

You may also cover a matt in fabric or marbled paper, mitering the corners neatly. Ideally, use a type of adhesive spray which will allow you to move the material or paper around before it is stuck forever!

## SIZING THE PICTURE

**I**t is important, before you cut your matt, to decide on the size of the window and what area of the picture you want to show. Many pictures benefit from being "cropped" in this way, drawing you into the focal point more immediately.

A photo of a presentation of a trophy, for example, may look far better with just the two people involved shown, rather than a lot of background. It is also a matter of taste; many posters incorporate wording at the bottom, perhaps giving the name of the artist, gallery, or exhibition. These often use a large amount of white paper below the picture which some people like, but others prefer to take out.

To help you decide on the area, either cut a pair of "masks" – two L-shaped pieces of cardboard – (ensure they are square), approximately 2 inches wide and long enough to accommodate, say, a picture of 16in x 20in or four straight strips of cardboard so you can build up a "frame". Placing them on the picture will allow you to adjust the size of the window, while framing the area you wish to show. Remember that not all pictures have to be rectangular. Accentuating the picture's narrowness or width you can create a far more interesting and attractive result.

OPPOSITE: Sample color matts cut as L-shaped "masks" for sizing the picture with a finished double matt.
NEXT PAGE: A selection of attractive oval-cut matts.

### CUTTING THE MATT

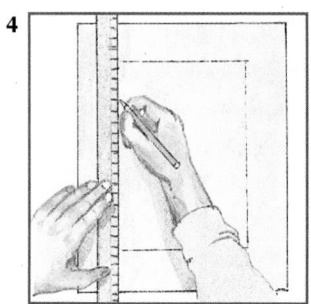

O nce you have established and noted the size of the window, you must decide on the width of the border. On average, for balance, two or three inches will be sufficient, although some pictures will lend themselves to wider matts. Sometimes, the smallest picture can look effective in a larger matt, while a large poster may not require one at all.

Cutting the window of the matt is not quite as easy as it looks and it is quite difficult to cut a bevel with a trimming- or craft-knife. However, it can be done with practice. The ideal is a matt-cutter designed for the job which has a blade set at an angle of about 60°. The cutter can also be adjusted for boards of different depths and some include a rule with runner grooves to guide you.

Usually, the top and the sides of the matt are of equal width but the bottom is about one-fifth deeper for it to look balanced. For example, the top and the sides could be $2\frac{3}{4}$in and the bottom 3in.

1 Do not presume the matt board is square to start with. Use a set-square to check.

2 Cut the board to the size you need with a trimming-knife (you do not need a bevel for the outside of the matt).

**Cut against the vertical edge of a steel rule, not against its bevel edge, and right on the line drawn with the pencil.**

3 Decide on the width of each border, then add each measurement to the corresponding dimensions of the window and mark the overall width and height of the matt on the back of the board.

**You should always mark and cut the matt board from the back. Erasing pencil lines on the front surface of the board could leave an ugly mark.**

4 Mark the dimensions of the window in pencil. If you are going to cut the bevel with a trimming-knife, a type with snap-off blades is best. Be careful, once you have cut the board, the edges can be extremely sharp.

5 The tip of the blade should be placed just to the outside edge of the pencil line so you can see as you cut. Cut against the beveled side of the steel rule, holding the knife at what you judge to be an angle of 60°. The pencil line should be visible on the edge of the cut out window – the center part.

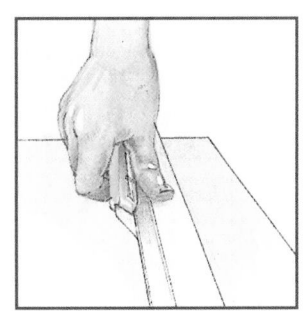

6 Push the tip of the blade into the full depth of the board, starting at the top of the line you are cutting, and then, with a tense arm, pull the blade down the length of the line toward your body. Remove the knife cleanly from the board.

7 Turn the board 90° and repeat the procedure for the next cut. You should finish the cut slightly beyond the point where the lines cross each other.

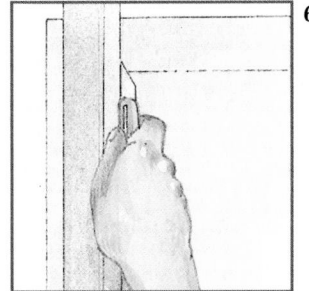

8 When you have made all four cuts, the center should drop out cleanly. It may not always do this immediately, so you may need to re-insert the blade, or use an artist's scalpel to nick each corner to release the center. Eventually, you will be able to judge when and where to stop each cut for the center to come away cleanly.

Cutting oval or round bevelled matts is a little harder, although if you have a bevel matt-cutter it will be somewhat easier. Professionals use a special piece of equipment.

You could however, use a dish, platter, or similar household item as a guide. Use it to make a template and then use this to cut around. You will need to practice to achieve a smooth curve.

You can buy ready-cut oval and circular matts as well as prepared matts for framing a number of pictures together – for example, sets of postcards or family photographs.

NEXT PAGE: An attractive selection of completed decorative matts and frames.

### MOUNTING PICTURES

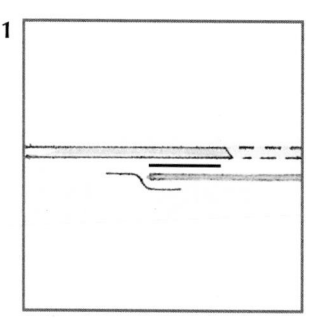

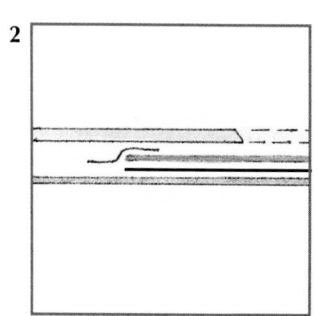

If you want to avoid your pictures wrinkling inside the frame, you will need to secure them to a light cardboard in some way. Here are just a few variations.

### Method One

Dry-mounting uses a special adhesive sheet, sandwiched between the artwork and the matt cardboard – usually white 1/32in cardboard. Specially-treated release paper is used with each sheet to protect the face of the picture from the heat.

Always ensure the picture is completely clean and free from dust and grease, or bubbles and tiny dents can appear.

Bonding takes place when the press reaches the correct temperature, sealing the artwork and the cardboard together.

Run strips of acid-free tape around the perimeter of the picture attached to the matt for long term strength.

1 Most professionals choose to "dry-mount" pictures which are not originals to the back of the matt – using a special dry-mount press.

2 Alternatively "dry-mount" pictures to a separate backing cardboard, then position the matt over the picture.

### Method Two

You can utilize the adhesive sheets without a dry-mount press using a warm iron.

3 Cut the adhesive sheet to the same size as the picture, place it on the back of the picture and, lifting the picture away for a moment, touch the adhesive sheet in the center with a warm iron so it attaches to the back of the picture.

4 Place this – with the picture face up in position on the backing-cardboard – and again lightly touch the adhesive sheet with a warm iron to attach it to the cardboard.

**Just attach it at one point only as more may cause bubbling.**

5 Then place the protective sheet over the picture and iron gently from the center. Keep the iron very cool to start with, working up to the correct temperature to bond the picture in position.

Dry-mount presses vary in size. If you use a small 13in x 16in area press, it will be necessary to reposition the picture within the press several times to cover the total area.

**Method Three**

You may also make a hinged matt, using a piece of cardboard the same size as the already-cut matt.

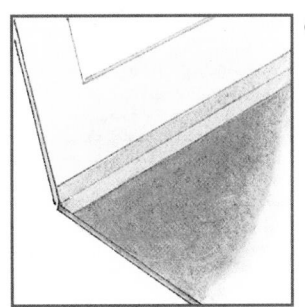

6 Trim a piece of cardboard the same size as the cut matt, lay the two together on a flat surface, and run a strip of masking tape across the join so that the matt hinges open.

7 Place the picture between the hinged, already-cut matt and backing-cardboard. Position the picture accurately within the matt window.

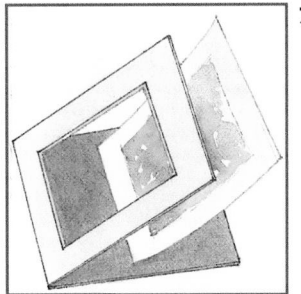

8 Ideally, use two small pieces of gummed, acid-free tape which will not mark the original artwork, and stick them to the back of the artwork so they extend slightly. Then secure these crosswise to the backing cardboard with either masking or gummed tape .

**Another alternative, although not recommended, is to glue the picture to the backing cardboard. However, beware using anything too wet (such as wallpaper paste) which can soak into the picture and cause it to bubble or damage it more severely. Cans of "spray-mount" are more suitable.**

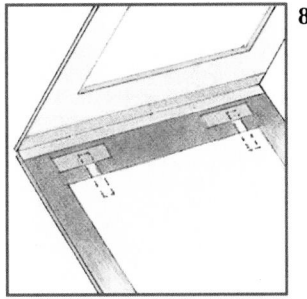

## BUYING AND CUTTING GLASS

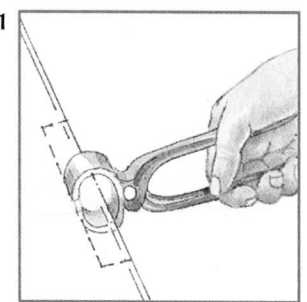

1

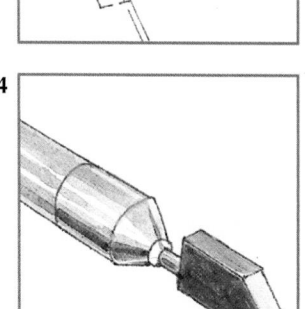

4

Glass is usually sold in sheets which can be rather awkward to handle and store but most suppliers will sell cut sheets and will deliver them to you for a charge.

You may prefer to have glass cut to size by a local glass-supplier. If you do, measure the area of the frame into which the picture will fit exactly and the glass cutter will make the correct allowance for a comfortable fit, or ideally take the frame, matt, and picture with you.

There are several types of glass available, the most widely used being $1/16$in paper float. You may occasionally find a use for non-reflective glass which is more expensive than paper float and has the unfortunate effect of dulling the picture slightly. Its main advantage is that it enables you to look at the picture instead of yourself if the picture is hung in a brightly-lit room.

1 Trying to fit a piece of glass into a frame which is slightly too small can lead to a nasty accident later when the glass cracks from too much pressure. It is also an awfully tricky job trimming a slim strip of glass from an already cut piece, although it can be done by nibbling it away with special glass (grozling) pliers.

It is quite easy to cut your own glass once you have the knack although even the experts have their disasters!

2 Ensure you have a flat surface wide enough to take the full size of the sheet of glass – none should extend over the edge or you will be unable to cut correctly.

3 You can only cut glass in straight complete lines; it is not possible to turn corners in one single cut.

4 You will need a glass-cutter, either with a tungsten wheel containing lubricating oil in the handle helping it run more smoothly, or a cutter which has to be lubricated by dipping it regularly into a sponge pad containing cutting-oil or white spirit. The latter will not last quite so long and does not have such a good cutting edge.

5 Make sure you have a completely clean surface to work on, perhaps with some cushioning of newspaper or felt under a heavy cardboard working surface, and mark the size needed on the glass with a fine felt-tip pen or colored chinagraph (wax) pencil. It is a good idea to practice the technique first on small pieces of glass rather than waste larger pieces.

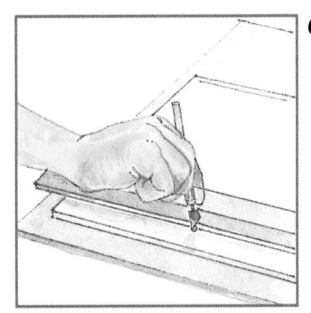

6 Use a long steel ruler to cut against and ensure the cutter is exactly on the line you have drawn. You will not be cutting right through the glass, simply scoring it.

**Let the wheel of the cutter run, keeping your fingers straight, pressing firmly and continuously, starting at the top of the line and drawing it down toward you. The pressure should come from your shoulder, not your wrist.**

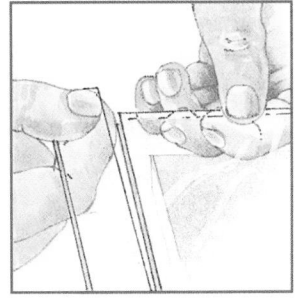

**You will be able to hear it scoring the surface and the noise should sound fluid rather than crunchy; the latter indicates you are using too much pressure and crushing the glass.**

7 The technique now is to break the glass cleanly along the line. Pull the glass over the edge of the table enough to get a grip with your thumbs, one each side of the cut line.

The thumbs should almost touch each other and your fingers should be underneath the glass. Lift the glass up slightly – half an inch or so – and at the same time, twist your hands away from each other, pushing up with the two fingers under the glass. Watch the glass split – hopefully – down the line.

## CUTTING THE BACKBOARD

Probably the easiest task is cutting the hardboard backing. You should use 1/16in hardboard for the backboard, ideally a new type called SBS (smooth both sides) which is half the thickness of ordinary hardboard. Although not generally available, it can be bought from framing suppliers. It can be cut with a trimming-knife or a miter-saw if you find it easier.

Do not try to cut right through with a knife – just score it, then snap it, using a fine rasp to tidy up the edges.

If you cut the hardboard with a saw, smooth the edges down with some sandpaper, or again use a fine rasp.

The hardboard backing should fit snugly into the back of the frame and be pinned in as part of the sandwich at the very end of the process. Before doing this the fittings for the backing should be attached (see page 35).

On some occasions, particularly if the rabbet of the frame is shallow, it may be necessary to chamfer the edges and drive the pins or staples into the frame at an angle (see page 32).

Y ou now have the four lengths of mitered molding, the beveled matt, the glass, the back-board, and the mounted picture.

T he next step is to make up the frame. Double-check that everything is going to fit within the frame first by making it up as a "dummy" run.

BELOW: Bring all the elements together for final assembly.

### MAKING UP THE FRAME

Professional framers use an expensive piece of equipment called an underpinner. It employs air pressure to shoot pins into the frame from the back to reinforce the corners. However, the home-framer will use panel pins which are hammered into the sides of the frame.

Do not put the pins in from the top or bottom of the frame as the weight of the glass, matt, and backing may be too great, and may force the frame apart.

You will need two pins at each corner (unless the frame is too narrow and there is only room for one) so it is recommended that you drill the holes for the pins first, using a narrow bit in a hand-drill so that the pin is a tight fit. Only drill the upright leg, not the leg the pin is being driven into.

**It is advisable to glue and pin the corners as you go.**

1 Take length 1 (long) and length 3 (short) and check that the mitered corners fit neatly together. Pre-drill the holes for the pins in the upright leg and knock the pins in halfway.

2 Smear a touch of wood-glue on the two mitered faces. Clamp the first leg in position. Then, putting the two faces together and ensuring the joint is good, clamp the second leg in place. Wipe off any excess glue that squeezes out.

3 Hit the pins home using a small hammer and, using a nail-set, punch them so they disappear just below the surface of the wood. Later, you can fill the dent with wood-filler or wax which can be retouched with matching paint on a very thin brush, or even a water-based, colored pencil. Leave to set.

4 Do the same with lengths 2 and 4. Then repeat the process with 1 and 4, and 2 and 3.

5 You will need four corner-clamps to hold the corners in the correct position. If you only have one or two clamps, you can do it in stages.

To hold the complete frame firmly, use a tape clamp. Ensure this fits straight and holds the frame without twisting. Use the winder which is incorporated in one of the corners to wind the tape so that it holds the corners firmly.

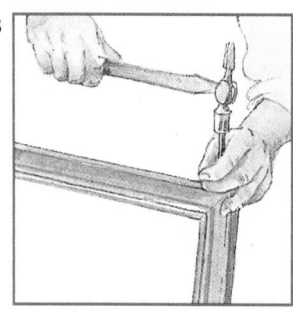

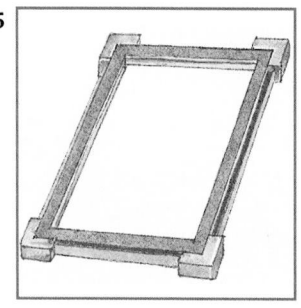

## FINAL ASSEMBLY

Having given the frame plenty of time for the glue to set, make sure your working area is clean. The first task is to carefully clean the glass. There is nothing more infuriating than putting together a picture which you then find has a large speck of dust just behind the glass!

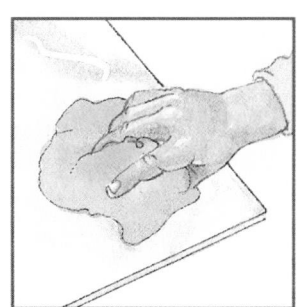

1 Rest the glass on a piece of felt or similar smooth cloth, use a glass-cleaning spray to clean both sides carefully with a soft lint-free cloth or paper towel (it is dust-free, disposable, and inexpensive), ensuring there are no smears.

2 Brush any loose chippings or sawdust out of the rabbet of the frame and any specks of dust you can see on the matt or picture itself.

3 Find a shallow box, smaller than the overall picture. Place the picture with the attached matt, then the glass (taking care to place the glass on the picture directly rather than pushing it across) then the frame on top, gently adjusting it all into the correct position. Turn the thing over and place the hardboard backing into the recess.

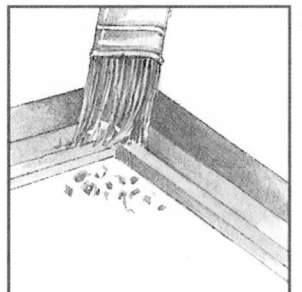

**Use either of the following methods to attach the hardboard backing to the frame.**

4 Professional framers use a staple-gun which shoots flat, metal, diamond- or arrow-shaped pins into the inside edge of the frame, pressing the hardboard to the rest of the picture sandwich and holding it all in place.

5 Alternatively, you can hammer in fine panel-pins. They need to be driven into the inside edge of the frame with a hammer, so that the length of the pin slides across the backing board, sandwiching it tightly.

Whichever method you use, do not scrimp on pins; use several along each length at regular intervals.

As they are inserted, hold a heavy weight (a padded wooden block or lead weight) against the outside edge of the frame to absorb the shock waves.

**If it is not possible for the back-board to fit flush into the frame, chamfer the edges of the board so that you can drive the pins into the frame at an angle.**

## THE FINISHING TOUCH

Once you have pinned the frame together, there is some tidying up to do.

1 Cover the pins holding the back of the frame with strips of either self-adhesive brown paper tape or masking tape, mitering the corners for neatness.

A craft-knife is the best way of cutting the tape – just a nick to the corner gives you a nice neat edge. The tape will also help to keep out dust and insects.

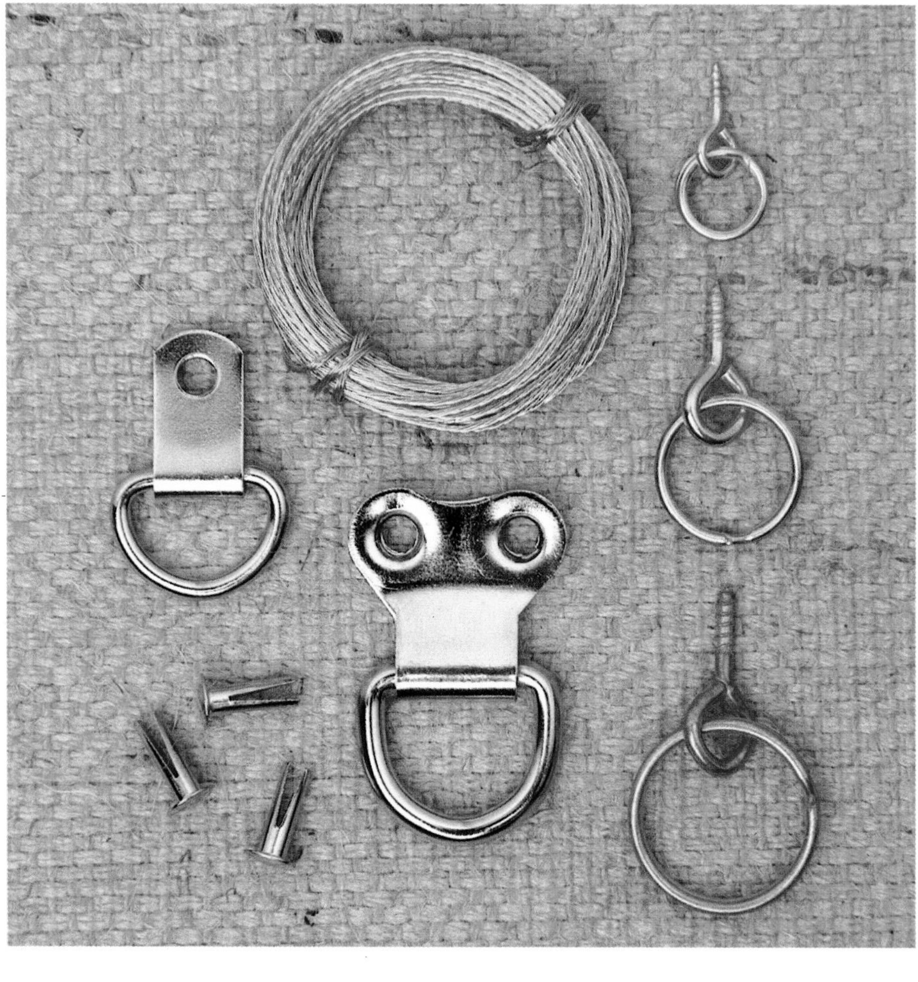

## HANGING METHODS

Which fastenings you use to hang your picture depends on its size. Two screw-eyes and a length of nylon cord will not be adequate to support a large poster but perfectly suitable for a small (10in x 8in) watercolor.

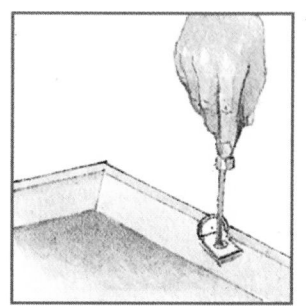

The best type of fittings are D-rings which are riveted to the backboard about a fifth of the way in from the side of the frame. Alternatively, screw-eyes with a ring for the cord or wire are screwed to the frame but may not be suitable for very narrow frames.

1 Position the fittings about a third of the way down from the top of the picture (D-rings should be fitted to the backboard before your final assembly of the picture) but can also be riveted to the frame.

2 Take a length of picture-hanging wire or nylon cord and run it between the D-rings or screw-eyes, allowing a little take-up (not too much) by pushing the wire upward with your finger at the center point to approximately two inches from the top of the picture.

3 Tie a double knot through one D-ring and run the wire across to the other D-ring.

4 Return the wire across, twisting the two lengths together to strengthen the cord. Secure the twisted wire through the D-ring at the other end.

The wall fixing could be as simple as a picture hook or nail, although once again it depends on the size of the picture and to some extent the type of wall. For larger pictures, it is safer to use an anchor and screw or masonry nail if you are attaching a hook to an outside brick or an internal load-bearing wall.

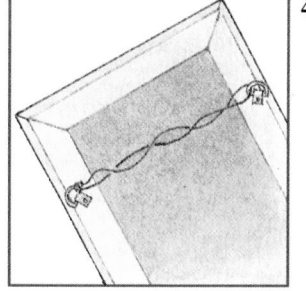

OPPOSITE: A selection of fastenings for hanging.

## HANGING PICTURES CREATIVELY

Give some careful thought to your picture display. A small picture hung in the center of a large wall will look totally lost.

You may feel that the pictures you hang are likely to stay in one place for some time or at least until the room is redecorated, but it is worth considering having the flexibility to change them around or replace them with new ones. Grouping pictures together allows you to do this.

Do not dismiss the more unusual rooms of the house. The bathroom, the kitchen, and the cloakroom all deserve enlivening and often have unusually-shaped areas where a picture will fit neatly.

However, beware of hanging delicate watercolors or oils in steamy places, such as near the bathtub or shower, or in the kitchen. They could be damaged by the humidity.

Other unusual places include over doorways, on the backs of doors, under sloping roofs (as long as it is bright enough) and in recesses alongside chimney breasts.

You can hang a picture alone (if it is striking enough) complemented by the furniture around it – why not place it on an easel, on a mantelpiece, or in a recess?

There is no need for a pair of pictures to be on the same theme although this can work. If you treat them similarly, with the same frame and matt, they can hang together very well.

No need for them to be hung exactly side by side, either. One a third higher than the other, with about a third of the width between them, will balance nicely. A table positioned centrally beneath gives more symmetry.

Nor is there any reason why pictures of different shapes, even ovals, cannot be hung together in a group.

If you take a line as eye-level, try and arrange the pictures centered along this line or above and below it. Alternatively, you can take an imaginary square, cross, or rectangle and build the pictures within this.

Ideally, keep larger pictures at the top of the arrangement and smaller pictures below where they can be seen more easily.

OPPOSITE ABOVE: A wall covered with pictures can look stunning.
OPPOSITE BELOW: Creative picture-hanging on a sloped wall adds interest to a room.

Elizabeth Whiting Associates

Elizabeth Whiting Associates

# *Home Workshop*
# CREATIVE FRAMING

A few simple but effective framing variations.

## DECORATIVE MATTS

There are many ways to decorate a basic matt but you can also add a complementary touch by picking out a color from your picture in a second matt which slips beneath the main matt to make a slim, colored border.

## CUTTING A DOUBLE MATT

**1** Cut the window to fit the picture in the first matt using colored cardboard.

**2** Select a second piece of cardboard in a complimentary color to the first and trim the outside measurements to exactly the same as the first.

**3** Cut out the second matt's window around a 1/4in larger than for the first matt. This measurement can vary, either smaller or larger, depending on your taste.

**The middle section of the first matt can be dropped onto the marked-out second matt to check that both are square and that the width is equal all the way around.**

**4** Cut out the window of the second matt and place the frame on top of the first matt.

**5** Using double-sided tape, carefully stick the two matts together to finish the completed double matt.

**You can use the same procedure for making a triple matt – perhaps varying the width of the third matt – but check that the depth of the rabbet on the frame is deep enough to accommodate them all!**

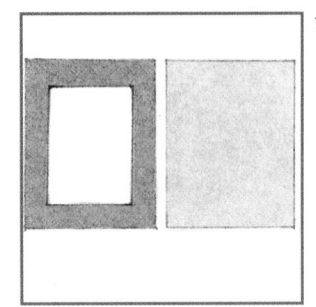

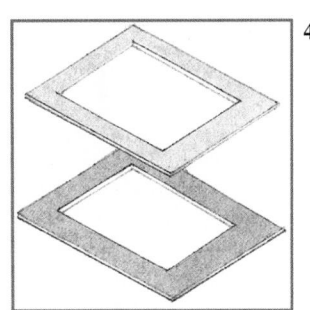

### CUTTING A V-GROOVE BORDER

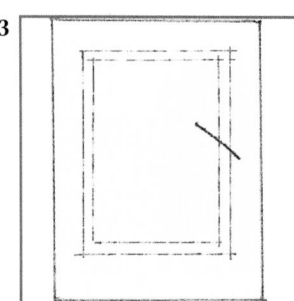

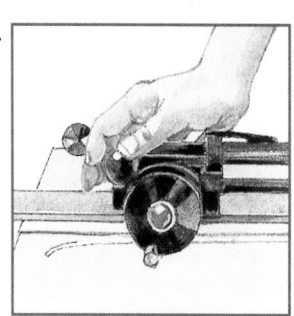

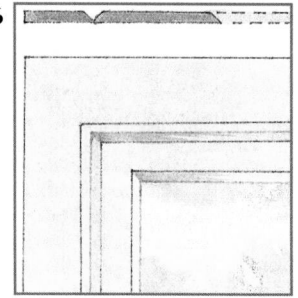

Ne popular way to decorate a matt is to cut a V-groove. Cut the overall size of the matt cardboard as you would for a single matt.

**1** Draw on the back the size you need for the final window – say 2in at the top and sides but 3in at the bottom.

**2** Then draw another rectangle around that, half an inch (or whatever you decide) closer to the outside edge – 1½in at the top and sides and 2½in at the bottom.

**3** Draw a pencil line on the back from the edge to near the center so you can replace the cut-out piece the same way up, using the pencil line as a guide for re-positioning.

**4** Cut the outside window first, which forms the cut for the V-groove. Drop the window out, turn it over, face up, and cut the bevel at the same angle as you did from the back. Be careful not to cut too much off.

**V-grooves are better cut with the proper hand tools.**

**5** Replace the center piece inside the matt, face down, ensure the pencil line you drew aligns on both pieces, and tape the two together at the back, using masking tape.

**6** Cut the final window which will frame your picture. The result will be the nice effect of a V-groove half an inch away from the picture.

## DECORATIVE RULES AND BORDERS

A nother way of adding a border is to use a ruling-pen, filled with gold-colored or other colored paint.

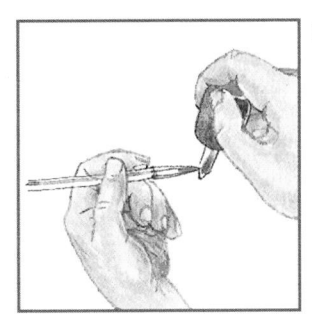

1

1 Use a pen which allows you to adjust the thickness of the rule and which has a wide nib so you can hold enough ink. Draw your border lightly in pencil before attempting the real thing.

2 You can then fill the borders, using watercolor wash, applied with a sable brush.

If you want to experiment with this technique there is a kit available which uses powder rather than paint and has all you need to add wash-line decoration to your matts.

The kit includes a corner-gauge which enables you to decide where the rules will fall and accurately mark them out (see figure 1, page 42).

BELOW: A sample of matts with an effective use of rules and borders.

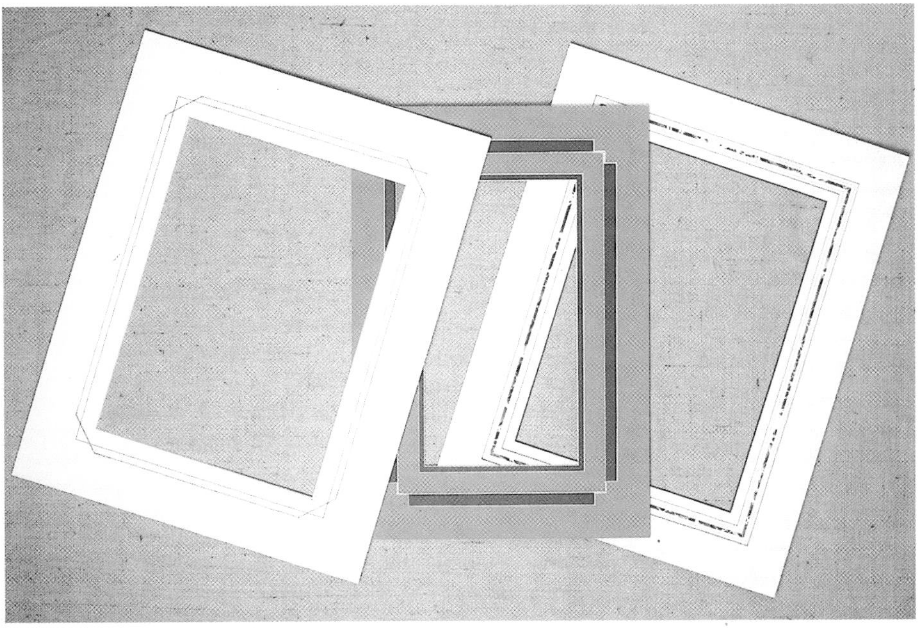

### A WASHED LINE MATT

**1**

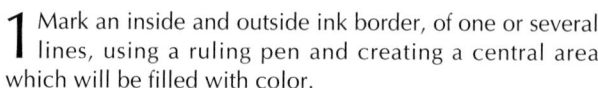

**1** Mark an inside and outside ink border, of one or several lines, using a ruling pen and creating a central area which will be filled with color.

**2** Using a straight edge (ruler) draw up the straight lines to link the marked out points.

**3** Using an artist's sable brush, load the brush with color and lightly guide a wet line wash evenly between the marked-up lines.

**If you are not sure about your drawing talent, there are plenty of other methods of decorating matts including matt-decoration papers.**

**2**

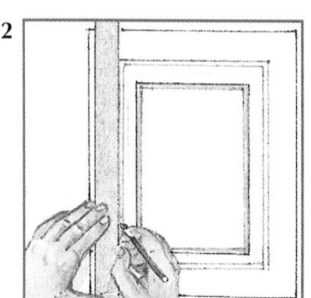

MATT-DECORATION PAPERS – are thin paper veneers which can be cut from sheets and stuck on with double-sided tape, or supplied with a self-adhesive backing in continuous rolls in a range of designs including marbled, wash and line, antique gold and silver, or plain pastels. Corner designs like stencils are also available in this self-adhesive format – or you could use a stencil kit and choose your own colors.

**3**

LEFT: A selection of ruled borders.

LEFT: A selection of decorative borders.

## DECORATIVE FRAMES

The introduction of plain wood frames has opened up all kinds of possibilities for decorative finishes.

You may wish to show the wood-grain off to its full advantage, either staining it with one of the wide range of water – or spirit-based – wood-stain colors that are now available, varnishing it, then brushing on a clear shellac to seal it and give a sheen or gloss finish depending on how many coats you apply.

Alternatively you can use paint to create some stippled or ragged effects using the same techniques as you would on walls or furniture.

For the more adventurous, it is not so difficult to re-create the effects of marble and tortoise shell which can look particularly stunning when used to frame mirrors and oil-paintings.

It is always helpful to have a sample of the marble or tortoise shell on hand (or a picture if the real thing is not available).

You will need:

PLAIN WOOD MOLDING – preferably not too grained or knotty.
UNIVERSAL PRIMER – or sanding sealer.
EGGSHELL PAINT.
WET-AND-DRY SANDPAPER.
ARTIST'S PAINTS.
CAN OF TRANSPARENT GLAZE.
BRUSHES – a selection including fitches, a hogshair softening brush, a Japanese Hakka and a small domed-sash or similar brush for tapping on paint.
MASKING TAPE.
ARTIST'S PALETTE – make your own with a piece of hardboard covered in parchment paper.

First prepare the frame with the universal primer (or sanding sealer). Build up several layers of eggshell paint (six should do it) and sand it down to a very smooth finish with wet-and-dry sandpaper.

Work on one leg of the frame at a time, covering the mitered corner with masking tape to ensure a clean line.

## MARBLING

The two artist's colors we suggest you start with are Payne's gray and raw umber, but you can vary these and add extra colors once you have perfected the technique.

1 Apply a very thin coat of transparent glaze to the first leg of the frame. Then "tap" on the gray using the domed-sash or other small brush evenly over the entire surface. Do not make it too dark.

2 Use the hogshair softening brush to soften the surface color – you will be surprised at how marble-like the effect is already.

3 If you do not like the effect in any particular area, dab it with a rag and soften again with the hogshair brush. Then "tap" the raw umber along the edges of the gray paint, picking out the shapes that suggest themselves. Skim gently over this with the hogshair brush and blend the two colors gently with a fitch brush.

4 To add the veins, use a fine pointed brush and trickle in the brown (raw umber) paint along routes which suggest themselves, such as the edges of the raw umber. Do not overdo it, but link the veins as you go along.

5 Splatter some white spirit onto the paint with a fitch to create some interesting teardrop effects and colorings.

BELOW: A selection of decorative frames including marbled and limed frames.

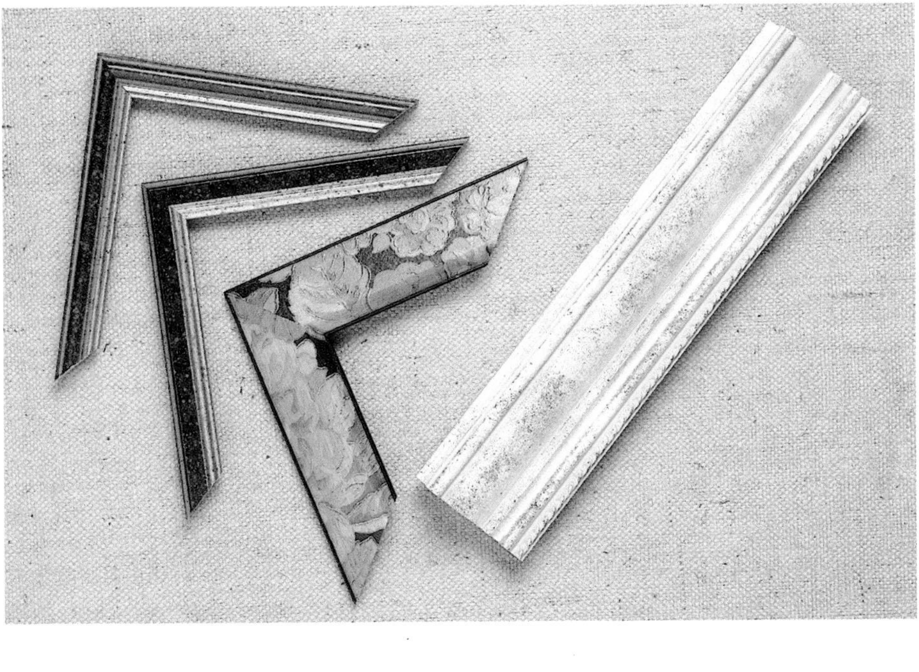

### TORTOISE SHELLING

Y ou can imitate the shell of a turtle (called tortoise shell) using a similar techniques.

1 Apply a thin coat of transparent glaze to the prepared frame.

2 Mix equal parts of raw sienna and yellow ocher with a touch of glaze.

3 Tap the color evenly onto the prepared frame with a stippling action. Do not make it too thick or the paint will streak when you soften it.

4 Mix some burnt umber with a touch of glaze. Add little dabs to the stippled base with a fitch brush. Imagine that you are painting little groups of grains – not quite touching each other.

5 A pattern begins to emerge – watch out for edges and open spaces.

6 Soften the edges with a hogshair softening brush, closing up the shapes where they appear.

7 Using the darker raw umber and with a second fitch brush, add highlights where they suggest themselves.

8 Soften the whole with a Hakka, which gives a smoother effect than that of the hogshair softening brush.

**A wide range of other effects can be achieved and you can take classes in these techniques if this sort of decoration appeals to you. You can re-create malachite, lapis lazuli, birds-eye maple, and red leather to name but a few.**

# ACKNOWLEDGMENTS

Photographic props supplied by:

Nina Barough Styling

As credited, photographic material reproduced by kind permission of:

Elizabeth Whiting Associates